ACTS 1–12

Part 1: God's Power in Jerusalem & Judea

12 STUDIES FOR INDIVIDUALS OR GROUPS

LifeGuide®
BIBLE STUDIES

PHYLLIS J. LE PEAU

ivp

An imprint of InterVarsity Press
Downers Grove, Illinois

InterVarsity Press
P.O. Box 1400, Downers Grove, IL 60515-1426
ivpress.com
email@ivpress.com

©1992, 2002 by Phyllis J. Le Peau

InterVarsity Press® is the book-publishing division of InterVarsity Christian Fellowship/USA®, a movement of students and faculty active on campus at hundreds of universities, colleges and schools of nursing in the United States of America, and a member movement of the International Fellowship of Evangelical Students. For information about local and regional activities, visit intervarsity.org.

LifeGuide® is a registered trademark of InterVarsity Christian Fellowship.

All Scripture quotations, unless otherwise indicated, are taken from the Holy Bible, New International Version®. NIV®. Copyright ©1973, 1978, 1984 by International Bible Society. Used by permission of Zondervan Publishing House. All rights reserved.

Cover design: Cindy Kiple
Interior design: Jeanna Wiggins
Cover image: volcano eruption: © AZ68 / iStockphoto

ISBN 978-0-8308-3119-7 (print)
ISBN 978-0-8308-6208-5 (digital)

Printed in the United States of America ∞

As a member of the Green Press Initiative, InterVarsity Press is committed to protecting the environment and to the responsible use of natural resources. To learn more, visit greenpressinitiative.org.

P	18	17	16	15	14	13	12	11	10	9	8	7	6	5	4	3	2	1
Y	33	32	31	30	29	28	27	26	25	24	23	22	21	20	19				

CONTENTS

GETTING THE MOST OUT OF *ACTS 1–12*

J ust before Acts begins, the disciples are wallowing in the mire of
their craven fear, self-doubt and personal shame. Apart from their
master, they are a pathetic group indeed (John 20:19; Luke 24:11). However,
by the second chapter of Acts, the same men who abandoned Jesus at
Gethsemane have become irrepressible dynamos, preaching with utter
conviction—and at great personal risk—"the mighty acts of God."

Acts is an important book for us today because it confirms that the
power of the Holy Spirit, which transformed the disciples' lives, is the
same power that can transform our lives today!

There are many benefits to studying Acts:

- *Acts serves as a distant mirror.* We see the dynamics of the earliest
  church, the nature of their fellowship, the intensity of their prayer
  life and their out-and-out zeal to declare the saving gospel of
  Jesus Christ. Our own situation will be called into question. What
  does it mean to be the church today?

- *Acts emphasizes the primary task of the church—evangelization.* In
  Acts we see the entire process of calling, healing, empowering and
  sending people forth to love and obey Jesus Christ.

- *Acts calls us to a vital experience with the Holy Spirit.* The book of
  Acts reveals the Holy Spirit as the driving force behind all mean-
  ingful ministry in Jesus' name.

- *Acts forges a new sense of identity.* The disciples gradually realized
  they were no longer Jews (at least from the confessional and ceremonial points of view). They slowly began to understand that
  they were part of that new community of the Spirit that was
  prophesied in the Hebrew Scriptures. And they saw the need to

call all people—Jews and Gentiles—to repentance and fellowship with this new community, the church.

Through these studies by Phyllis J. Le Peau, the explosive power of this living document will touch you. As you work through these studies, may you experience the calling, healing, empowering and sending dynamic of the Holy Spirit.

Louis Quetel

SUGGESTIONS FOR INDIVIDUAL STUDY

1. As you begin each study, pray that God will speak to you through his Word.

2. Read the introduction to the study and respond to the personal reflection question or exercise. This is designed to help you focus on God and on the theme of the study.

3. Each study deals with a particular passage—so that you can delve into the author's meaning in that context. Read and reread the passage to be studied. The questions are written using the language of the New International Version, so you may wish to use that version of the Bible. The New Revised Standard Version is also recommended.

4. This is an inductive Bible study, designed to help you discover for yourself what Scripture is saying. The study includes three types of questions. *Observation* questions ask about the basic facts: who, what, when, where and how. *Interpretation* questions delve into the meaning of the passage. *Application* questions help you discover the implications of the text for growing in Christ. These three keys unlock the treasures of Scripture.

Write your answers to the questions in the spaces provided or in a personal journal. Writing can bring clarity and deeper understanding of yourself and of God's Word.

5. It might be good to have a Bible dictionary handy. Use it to look up any unfamiliar words, names or places.

6. Use the prayer suggestion to guide you in thanking God for what you have learned and to pray about the applications that have come to mind.

7. You may want to go on to the suggestion under "Now or Later," or you may want to use that idea for your next study.

SUGGESTIONS FOR MEMBERS OF A GROUP STUDY

1. Come to the study prepared. Follow the suggestions for individual study mentioned above. You will find that careful preparation will greatly enrich your time spent in group discussion.

2. Be willing to participate in the discussion. The leader of your group will not be lecturing. Instead, he or she will be encouraging the members of the group to discuss what they have learned. The leader will be asking the questions that are found in this guide.

3. Stick to the topic being discussed. Your answers should be based on the verses which are the focus of the discussion and not on outside authorities such as commentaries or speakers. These studies focus on a particular passage of Scripture. Only rarely should you refer to other portions of the Bible. This allows for everyone to participate in in-depth study on equal ground.

4. Be sensitive to the other members of the group. Listen attentively when they describe what they have learned. You may be surprised by their insights! Each question assumes a variety of answers. Many questions do not have "right" answers, particularly questions that aim at meaning or application. Instead the questions push us to explore the passage more thoroughly.

When possible, link what you say to the comments of others. Also, be affirming whenever you can. This will encourage some of the more hesitant members of the group to participate.

5. Be careful not to dominate the discussion. We are sometimes so eager to express our thoughts that we leave too little opportunity for others to respond. By all means participate! But allow others to also.

6. Expect God to teach you through the passage being discussed and through the other members of the group. Pray that you will have an enjoyable and profitable time together, but also that as a result of the study you will find ways that you can take action individually and/or as a group.

7. Remember that anything said in the group is considered confidential and should not be discussed outside the group unless specific permission is given to do so.

8. If you are the group leader, you will find additional suggestions at the back of the guide.

ONE

YOU WILL BE
MY WITNESSES

Acts 1

I remember telling a friend, "If I were dying, what I would most need would be confidence that all I believed about Jesus was true."

During the days between his resurrection and ascension, Jesus built the confidence of his disciples. He demonstrated and spoke truth about himself. And then he left them with a clearly defined task and the promise of the power to carry out that task. Thus, Luke was able to write with confidence to Theophilus about Jesus.

Group Discussion. When has your faith in Jesus Christ been encouraged by the words of others?

Personal Reflection. I need confidence that everything I believe about Jesus is true, not only when I am dying but also when I am living. What do you need to build your confidence in who Jesus is?

In this study we will consider the task of building the church of Jesus Christ and his promise to equip us for that task. *Read Acts 1:1-11.*

1. What did Luke, the author of Acts, report to Theophilus about Jesus' last days on the earth?

2. What gives credibility to this report?

3. How is your hope and confidence in Jesus affected by what you learn of him in the passage?

4. Put yourself in the shoes of the apostles. How would you feel if you were the first to be given the task described in verse 8?

5. How are we equipped for this task, according to the passage?

6. Imagine that you were there, looking into the sky. How do you think the followers of Jesus were affected by the promise that he would return?

7. How are you affected by that promise today?

8. *Read Acts 1:12-26.* How did the disciples respond to all that they had seen and heard?

9. Why was it important for them to be together?

10. How are you affected when you pray with other believers in this way—especially as you consider your part in this task (v. 14)?

11. Peter comes forth as the leader of this group. He goes to Scripture immediately when he speaks. How do the words of David affect their confidence, as well as give them direction?

12. What do you find in this passage to equip, motivate and give you confidence to complete the task that has been set before you?

 Thank God for giving you the marvelous task of being his witness. Tell him about the fears and joys that you feel as his servant in this mission.

NOW OR LATER

Reflect on what it means for you to be Jesus' witness in Jerusalem, Judea, Samaria and the ends of the earth. Where is your Jerusalem—those closest to you who need to know Jesus? Your Judea—your nation? Your Samaria—those in your world who are different from you, for whom you would have to cross lines of culture and prejudice and move out of your comfort zone to love? What is your role in taking the good news to the ends of the earth? That is, how might you support world missions?

TWO

RECEIVING
THE POWER

Acts 2

At my school of nursing, a group of upperclassmen wanted to communicate the message of Jesus to the incoming class of freshmen. They realized that there was only one source to accomplish this task—the power of the Holy Spirit. So they decided to pray for each new student by name weeks before he or she arrived on campus. As a result, many who did not know Jesus when they arrived graduated as maturing Christians.

Group Discussion. What do you think it would be like if the Holy Spirit were suddenly withdrawn from the church?

Personal Reflection. Although at times we do not sense him, the Holy Spirit is always there to help us. Let him quiet you now and open your heart to what he wants to tell you about himself.

In this study we will look at the power of the Holy Spirit and how he equips us for the task of being witnesses throughout the world. *Read Acts 2.*

1. What highlights would a reporter who is at the scene on this day of Pentecost be likely to mention?

2. What would it feel like to be one of the disciples at this scene?

3. How do the Jews see the power of the Spirit demonstrated? How do they respond (vv. 5-13)?

4. The power of the Holy Spirit transformed Peter who was once a coward who denied Jesus. Scripture, again, is the foundation of Peter's proclamation of truth. What message do the book of Joel and the Psalms have for the bewildered crowd (vv. 17-35)?

5. In our study of Acts we will see Peter's perception of evangelism broaden. In this chapter why do you think there is a difference between the people Luke mentions as being present (vv. 9-11) and Peter's address, "Fellow Jews" (v. 14)?

6. What is there in Peter's sermon that would reassure Theophilus about his faith and help him "know the certainty of the things" that he'd been taught?

7. What reassurance(s) in Peter's message is most important to you as you consider being Jesus' witness?

8. What does Peter have to offer to those who are responsive to his message (vv. 37-39)?

9. How have your life and ministry been affected by the gift of the Holy Spirit?

10. Describe the fellowship of the believers in this young church, including their priorities (vv. 42-47).

11. What do you think it would be like for the Lord to add daily to the numbers of your Christian community those who are being saved?

12. How does the life and purpose of your church or Christian community compare to this group?

13. How does your church or Christian community need to change in order to experience the power of the Holy Spirit and to become a more effective witness?

 Ask God to make the power of the Holy Spirit come alive in you, and pray that he will use you through that power. Ask him to add to your community those who are being saved.

NOW OR LATER

Continue to reflect on the fellowship of the believers as described in this chapter. Rewrite the last paragraph (vv. 42-47), applying it to your specific situation today. For instance, what does it mean for you and your community to devote yourself to the apostles' teaching? to the fellowship? to the breaking of bread? to prayer? Continue in this way throughout the paragraph as you paraphrase it.

THREE

HEALING POWER

Acts 3

I met **Anne at the hospital** where I was working one evening. She was in an isolation room. She had hepatitis because she used contaminated needles to take drugs.

In time our relationship grew, and Anne came to know Jesus. She recovered from hepatitis and went off drugs. She worked at healing her relationship with her parents. Later, she married and established a Christian home.

Anne's story makes it clear that the power of the Holy Spirit is demonstrated not only through physical healing but also in the "complete healing" that includes every aspect of our lives.

Group Discussion. In your experience, what causes non-Christians to be open to hear about Jesus?

Personal Reflection. Recall a time when you felt broken and in need of healing. Thank God for the ways that he has transformed you and healed you since then.

In this passage our understanding of the power of God is deepened as we see it demonstrated in the healing of the crippled beggar. *Read Acts 3.*

| **1.** What caused the people to be filled with wonder and amazement?

| **2.** How does the response of the people to this miracle contrast with that of the beggar (vv. 8, 11-12)?

3. How do you usually respond to the amazing acts of God?

4. What is the significance of the fact that they found the crippled man at the temple gate?

5. When Peter saw the response of the crowd, he saw his opportunity and talked to them about Jesus. According to Peter's message, what had God done to Jesus (vv. 13-15)?

What had the Jews done to him?

6. How is the authority of Jesus demonstrated in this miracle (v. 16)?

7. What do you think it meant that "complete healing" (v. 16) was given to the beggar?

What healing do you need in your life?

8. How did Peter explain that all that had happened to Jesus was a part of God's plan (vv. 17-26)?

9. Focus on verse 21. The wait for Jesus to return from heaven may seem very long—but this verse gives us some perspective. What are your thoughts and feelings about waiting for Jesus to return?

10. To what extent does God's Word affect your confidence, actions and attitudes about God and life?

11. How do you respond when you have opportunities like Peter's to talk about Jesus?

12. In summary, how is the power of the Holy Spirit linked to the truth about Jesus in this passage?

13. The "completely" healed man was a powerful testimony to the power of God and the truth of Peter's words. How have you seen the power of God demonstrated in your life and in the lives of others?

 Thank God for working so powerfully to change your life, and ask him to give you the opportunity to talk about Jesus to one person this week.

NOW OR LATER

Peter and John made a point at being where the action was—in the place where those on the road to meeting Jesus were. How in your life might you be and serve where you would be apt to meet people who need Jesus? Ask for the direction and wisdom of the Holy Spirit, and make plans to meet or interact with not-yet Christians.

FOUR

CALLED INTO QUESTION

Acts 4:1-31

I n the midst of pain and injustice we long to see God change things in our lives and in our world. But sometimes this hope is challenged by cynicism or skepticism when God's power is clearly at work.

Group Discussion. When has your faith in Jesus Christ been challenged by others?

Personal Reflection. Today, in this new day that God has created, your Savior wants to come to you. With calmness let the distractions around you, the voices and restless thoughts, slip away. As the Spirit of God comes to dwell with you, allow yourself to enjoy his presence in quietness and gratitude.

A disabled person becomes abled! And a one-time burden to society, a beggar, becomes functional and a contributing citizen. Instead of expressing gratitude, the religious leaders become extremely upset. *Read Acts 4:1-22.*

| **1.** What upset the religious leaders, and how did they respond?

| **2.** Just a few weeks have passed since Annas and Caiaphas had been involved in the condemnation of Jesus. In his response to their question "By what power or what name did you do this?" Peter is forcing them to encounter Jesus again. What does Peter say about Jesus (vv. 10-12)?

3. How do you feel and how do you respond when you are challenged or criticized about your faith in Jesus?

4. In what ways does the church confront the world with Jesus Christ today?

How does the church fail to do this?

5. In verses 13-22, why was it so difficult for the opposing religious leaders to bring this unacceptable behavior to a halt?

6. How do these same things, when present in our Christian communities, enhance accomplishing the task of spreading the news about Jesus?

7. Imagine that you had been in a group of believers to whom John and Peter returned and told what had happened. What would have been your reaction?

8. *Read Acts 4:23-31.* What was the reaction of the believers to John and Peter's account?

9. What is the significance of their unity in the midst of their task and power being challenged?

10. What does their prayer tell you about their faith in the character, power and faithfulness of God?

11. What do your prayers communicate about your view of God?

12. What did they finally request of God in the last part of their prayer?

13. "After they prayed, the place where they were meeting was shaken. They were all filled with the Holy Spirit and spoke the word of God boldly" (v. 31). In what ways do you need the power of the Holy Spirit to face the world today?

 Ask God to fill you with the Spirit as you face constant challenge to the power for and the task of experiencing and communicating the gospel.

NOW OR LATER

Write a letter to God. Tell him about areas in your life and witness where you are stretched, criticized or challenged. Tell him where you need his strength and grace. Write specifically how you would like for your words and life to proclaim Jesus, raised from the dead. Ask him to make you a person of courage, proclaiming Jesus.

Write about specific places and ways that you would like to see this life of proclamation happen. In what ways would you like to faithfully obey God rather than human beings? Describe the kind of prayer partner or group that you would like for him to give you. Finally, tell him how you would like for your own prayer life to change and grow more like the prayers of those in this chapter.

FIVE

ONENESS OF HEART

Acts 4:32–5:16

I t was with a heavy feeling of dread and pain that I read name after name engraved on the Vietnam Memorial in Washington, D.C. Then I saw that next to the memorial stood a statue of three men—a black, a Hispanic and a white soldier—standing very close together.

The tour guide, a former soldier who fought in Nam, explained that more minorities fought for the United States there than ever before. In Vietnam soldiers learned how much they *needed each other.*

Group Discussion. When have you experienced the power of the Holy Spirit in your own life as a result of being at one with other believers?

Personal Reflection. Who has God given you to meet specific needs in your life recently? How have they met these needs? Take the time to write a note to express your gratitude to them.

In this study we will see that when the battle is spiritual, our need for each other is even more critical. *Read Acts 4:32–5:16.*

1. What examples of unity and division do you see in this passage?

2. What do you think it would be like for you to be a part of the kind of community described in verses 4:32-37 and 5:12-16?

3. What did Ananias and Sapphira do that was not consistent with Christian community (5:1-2)?

4. Pretend you are watching the interaction between Peter and Ananias and Sapphira (5:3-9). How would you report this incident?

5. According to 5:11, "Great fear seized the whole church and all who heard about these events." How do you think the church was affected by this fear?

6. How does this story demonstrate the high value that God places on truth and unity within the body of Christ?

7. In what ways do we lie to each other today within our Christian communities?

8. How does not telling the truth with each other bring about death, in a spiritual and emotional sense, within our community?

9. What are the tangible evidences of the power of the Holy Spirit in this community in 5:12-16?

10. Why do you suppose that no one dared to join the believers when they met together in Solomon's Colonnade?

11. What difference would it make in our witness to the world today if believers were "highly regarded by the people"?

12. What characteristics does your Christian community share with the believers in Acts?

How is it different?

13. How could you begin to help others in your church or fellowship understand what Christian community is about?

 Ask God to uphold truth in his church and to help you speak truth in love before others.

NOW OR LATER

Journal on the following questions: How do I testify to the resurrection of the Lord Jesus? What do I do to make sure there are no needy people in my community? How do I lie to my brothers and sisters in Christ? to non-Christians? What miracles have I witnessed?

SIX

PERSECUTION & EXPANSION

Acts 5:17–6:7

I n 1956 tragic news spread across the world. Five American men—sons, husbands and fathers—were massacred by a tribe of Auca Indians. Their purpose was to take the good news of Jesus Christ to the Aucas. The opposition to this endeavor cost them their lives.

That agonizing loss, which seemed at the time to be such a waste, has turned into great fruit for the kingdom of God. Over the years that same tribe of Indians has been transformed by the power of God. The message of Jesus was taken to them by the loved ones of those five young men. Another visible fruit of this great loss is the many who have gone into the world with the gospel, having been inspired by the lives and deaths of these missionaries. The church of Jesus Christ continues to expand today in spite of great persecution, even as it did in the day of the apostles.

Group Discussion. When have you encountered internal or external opposition when you have attempted to proclaim the message of Jesus? Which is more difficult for you to deal with? Why?

Personal Reflection. Although we know that God is in complete control of the universe, we often forget that he also has plans for our individual lives. Think about his sovereignty everywhere, including the secrecy of your own heart. How is this fact comforting to you? In what ways is it uncomfortable? What secrets of your heart do you wish God did not know?

In this study we will consider the inadequacy of opposition and persecution to thwart the growth of the church of Jesus Christ. *Read Acts 5:17-42.*

1. Describe the apostles' response, motivation and source of strength throughout this whole episode.

Witness + Holy Spirit;
Each other

2. In what ways do you need this kind of response, motivation or strength from the Holy Spirit in your life?

in the life of your Christian community?

3. What was Gamaliel's message to the religious leaders (vv. 34-39)?

If this is Not of God - it will fissel out
If it is - you will not be able to stop it

4. How was his influence in saving the apostles' lives an example of the truth of which he spoke?

Because it was of God - it has grown
thru time And word has spread throughout
the world

5. When have you been or might you be called on to speak truth in a situation where it might not be welcomed?

Meeting with Jeff

6. *Read Acts 6:1-7.* As the number of disciples increased, what practical needs began to present themselves?

The need to serve the Flock

7. How did the Twelve respond to these needs (6:2-6)?

Asked the people of the church to select those who the trusted and felt worthy

★ System we use today for selection of Elders + Deacons

8. How does this response demonstrate sensitivity to these needs and their commitment to God's primary direction to them?

9. How does this response to need compare and contrast to your Christian community?

10. What is the spirit of those who are involved in the work of God throughout this passage?

11. What is the response to the truth that is being lived and proclaimed?

12. As you observe the work of the Holy Spirit throughout these passages, what actions do you think you or your Christian community should take to insure his ministry among you?

 Pray that the Holy Spirit will impress deeply on your heart and mind the truth of the gospel. Tell God about the difficulties and struggles you have been facing as a believer in him. Ask him to help you to faithfully, boldly and sensitively proclaim and live out truth.

NOW OR LATER

Slowly reread the story in Acts 5:17-42. Do a character study of each of the individuals and groups. What do you see and learn? What motivates you? What serves as a warning for you? What comparisons and contrasts do you see between the story in this passage and the story in the introduction to this study? Now write the story in your own words—as if you were there.

SEVEN

SPIRIT & WISDOM

Acts 6:8–7:60

I am glad for those people in my life who make me long to know God better. God's character in them makes me hunger and thirst for him. That is what happens to me when I am exposed to Stephen. Stephen is described as "full of Spirit and wisdom, . . . full of God's grace and power" (Acts 6:3, 8). I read about him, and I want to know God.

Group Discussion. Describe someone you know who makes you want to know God better.

Personal Reflection. Think of a person who makes you want to know God better. Reflect on the qualities you see in that person and on why you are encouraged by them to want to know God better.

In this study we will look at God's Spirit and wisdom manifested in Stephen and seek to make them more a part of our lives. *Read Acts 6:8–7:60.*

1. What do you learn about Stephen throughout this passage?

2. What would it have been like for you if you were Stephen?

3. Describe what you think it was like for the religious leaders not to be able to stand up against Stephen's wisdom or the Spirit by whom he spoke.

4. What do the accusations against Stephen tell us about why the Jewish religious leaders were so upset (6:13-14)?

5. Sometimes the speech in chapter 7 is called "Stephen's defense," although it is actually a defense of pure Christianity as God's appointed way to worship. What are the main points of this defense?

6. What did God tell Abraham would happen to his descendants, the Hebrews (7:1-7)?

7. All that God told Abraham would happen to the Hebrews did unfold in history. What response do you have as you ponder this?

8. What statement is Stephen making about where God can be worshiped in 7:44-50?

9. What direct application does Stephen make concerning the religious leaders from 7:39-43 (see also 7:51-53)?

10. How did God directly minister to Stephen as he faced the angry leaders and his own death?

11. Throughout this whole passage we see in Stephen the evidence of being full of the Spirit and wisdom. What are the evidences today of being full of the Spirit and wisdom?

12. In what aspect of your life would you like to reflect more of the Spirit and wisdom?

 Ask God to fill you with his Holy Spirit and wisdom.

NOW OR LATER

There are many important details in Stephen's defense. Outline chapter 7 as if you were preparing to write a paper on it. After you finish the outline write about the points that impact you the most, including why each is important to you.

EIGHT

THE POWER
OF SUFFERING

Acts 8

S tephen is dead. When he is buried, the people mourn deeply. The
church has experienced the tragedy of the first martyr. Persecution
of the church continues but so does expansion throughout the world.

Group Discussion. What do you feel you need to do to become a more
effective witness for Jesus?

Personal Reflection. When have you been confused about God's inten-
tions behind the events that he placed in your life? Ask him to give you
his understanding and peace.

In this study we meet Philip and Saul. Saul is putting all his energy into
destroying the rest of Jesus' followers. In contrast, Philip is full of the
Spirit and wisdom. His energy goes into the proclamation of the truth
about Jesus. *Read Acts 8.*

1. The command to be witnesses in all of Judea and Samaria
(Acts 1:8) is fulfilled. What are the causes and extent of the spread
of the gospel at this time?

2. How are you seeing the command to be witnesses fulfilled in your
life and community?

3. How does the power of the Holy Spirit continue to be demonstrated?

4. Look at the story of Simon the sorcerer (vv. 9-25). How does he attempt to get spiritual power?

What is his motivation for wanting this power (vv. 18-19)?

5. In contrast, what is God's way for his people to receive spiritual power (vv. 20-23)?

6. In what ways do you attempt to receive spiritual power?

7. The story of Simon the sorcerer demonstrates that becoming a Christian does not instantly resolve all problems and character flaws. What do you learn from Peter concerning nurturing young believers?

What results do you see in Simon?

8. What are the factors involved in the eunuch's coming to know the Lord (vv. 26-39)?

9. How was Philip's ministry to the eunuch the beginning of the witness "to the ends of the earth" (Acts 1:8)?

10. What do you see as your opportunities and responsibilities for taking the gospel to the ends of the earth?

11. Today we refer to different kinds of evangelism, such as friendship evangelism, mass evangelism, door-to-door evangelism and literature evangelism. What kinds of evangelism do you see in this passage?

12. What principles of evangelism have you observed throughout this study?

13. What have you learned from this passage that might make you a more effective witness for Jesus?

 Ask God for the guidance of the Holy Spirit, for ears to hear his voice and a heart that obeys. Confess times when you have tried to receive spiritual power in ways not pleasing to him.

NOW OR LATER

Take time to journal on the topic of suffering. First, write a paragraph on the four or five most painful times in your life. In each paragraph include a brief description of the situation and the cause for the suffering. Now do the same concerning several times that you have witnessed suffering in other believers. Finally, read through what you have written. Then write what you have seen of God in the suffering.

NINE

SAUL'S CONVERSION

Acts 9:1-31

W hen **Chuck Colson became a Christian**, the whole nation reacted with skepticism—Christians and non-Christians alike. Of all the leading characters in the Watergate scandal, he was one of the most notorious. Could such a calculating man sincerely come to God?

Group Discussion. Whose conversion to Christianity has been most astonishing to you? Why?

Personal Reflection. Think back to what your life was like before you met Christ. Thank God for the transformation that he has made in you—both your instant rebirth into his kingdom and the gradual remolding of your character since then.

In this study we will consider God's miraculous work in Saul's conversion and the effect of this on the whole church. *Read Acts 9:1-31.*

1. Review what you know about Saul (7:58–8:3). What further insights do you get about him from 9:1-2?

2. Describe Saul's encounter with Jesus Christ in verses 3-9. What is the emotional, spiritual, physical and social climate?

3. How does your conversion compare and contrast with that of Saul's?

4. Ananias is the second person within three days to have a direct encounter with the Lord. Compare and contrast his encounter (vv. 10-16) with that of Saul.

5. What is the significance of Ananias addressing Saul as "brother" (v. 17)?

6. What do you learn about obedience to God through Saul and Ananias?

7. What does Saul's conversion teach us about those in our lives who are most likely *not* to believe?

8. Consider the people in your life who are most antagonistic to Christianity. How might God use you to bring them to Christ?

9. What is the response of both believers and nonbelievers to Saul and his ministry (vv. 19-30)?

10. What role does Barnabas play in Saul's life and ministry?

11. Barnabas means "Son of Encouragement" (4:36). When have you experienced someone being a Barnabas to you or you to another?

12. How would you like to grow as a person who communicates the gospel to those who are antagonistic to it?

Begin praying and continue to pray faithfully for someone that you consider an unlikely convert. Ask God to grow your faith and to do a work of redemption in this person. Ask him to prepare you for being involved in this person's life.

NOW OR LATER

Think about when you met Christ and became his follower. Write a description of what you were like before you turned your life over to him. Describe what transformation took place instantly. Finally, describe the more gradual transformation that has taken place and that you want to see take place.

TEN

SALVATION FOR EVERY NATION

Acts 9:32–10:48

Once the Berlin Wall seemed impenetrable, and communism powerful and indestructible. For seventy years, Christians wondered if Christmas would ever again be openly celebrated.

Then, dramatically, the wall fell. Communism collapsed. Nations that had been closed to the gospel for years began to welcome Christians, their help and their message with open arms.

The historic breakthrough was like the one the early Christians experienced in this passage. A seemingly impenetrable spiritual wall was broken down. In both situations we see that from God's perspective there is always the potential for reaching every person in all corners of the world with the wonderful news of Jesus Christ.

Group Discussion. When have you felt separated from people because of cultural or racial differences?

Personal Reflection. Who in your world of relationships is most unlike you? How is your communication with that person affected by these differences?

Our aim in this study is to increase our understanding of the potential of the gospel to reach every person in each corner of the world. *Read Acts 9:32–10:48.*

| **1.** How is God's power demonstrated throughout this passage?

2. The experience with Tabitha is the first time Peter has been involved in raising someone from the dead. How might this help
prepare him for what happens in chapter 10?

3. When have you obeyed more quickly because of seeing God's
work and faithfulness in a previous situation?

4. How did God prepare Cornelius for Peter (10:1-8)?

5. According to 10:4, what caused God to take notice of Cornelius?

6. To what extent are prayer and giving to the poor priorities for you?

7. In what ways did God prepare Peter for Cornelius (10:9-33)?

8. What evidence is there that Cornelius expected God to work (10:24-26)?

9. What lessons do you learn from Cornelius's life?

10. Throughout the chapter, we see Peter in process concerning God's desire for him to take the gospel to the Gentiles. Trace the process of Peter's understanding.

11. What would have been the consequences if Cornelius or Peter had not obeyed God?

12. In summary, how do you see God's purpose, as stated in Acts 1:8—"You will receive power when the Holy Spirit comes on you; and you will be my witnesses in Jerusalem, and in all Judea and Samaria, and to the ends of the earth"—being fulfilled in this passage?

13. In what ways do you need to grow in relating to people of other cultures and races?

 Ask God to make you open to get to know, to love and to share your relationship with Jesus with people of other ethnicities and cultures.

████████████████████ NOW OR LATER ████████████████████

The group discussion and personal reflection sections ask you to begin to think about your relationship with people who are different from you. Continue that process now by dividing a sheet of paper into four columns. In the first column list ten people in your life who are significantly different (in ethnicity, culture, religious beliefs, gender and so on) from you. In the second column jot down how you are affected by the way you are different. In the third column write what you can do to enhance the relationship. In the fourth column write what God can teach you from this relationship.

ELEVEN

THE FIRST JEWISH-GENTILE CHURCH

Acts 11

L uke set up the stories of Peter and Cornelius and Ananias and Saul with amazing symmetry. The Holy Spirit simultaneously prepared the heart of Ananias and of Saul—as he simultaneously prepared those of Peter and Cornelius. Peter questioned and hesitated, as did Ananias. Peter doubted whether he could be friends with the Gentiles, Ananias whether he could approach the enemy of the church. Both obey without hesitation when God makes his divine will known.

These stories come together in today's study. Peter defends his ministry to Cornelius to the church at Jerusalem. He convinces them of God's work in the Gentiles. It is also here that Saul, that one-time enemy of the church, reappears as a *minister* to the church in Antioch, a church filled with both Jew and Gentile Christians.

Group Discussion. When have you been criticized by other Christians for doing what was right?

Personal Reflection. Think about times that you have been criticized. What was it like for you?

In this passage we will observe how the church is progressing from a Jewish church separate from the Gentiles to a Jewish-Gentile fellowship. *Read Acts 11.*

1. What kind of reception was awaiting Peter when he went back up to Jerusalem?

2. What are you like when someone criticizes you?

3. What can we learn from the way Peter responded to his critics?

4. What seemed to be the final and most convincing proof to Peter of God's working in the Gentiles (vv. 15-17)? Why?

5. What kinds of evidence of new life do you look for in new believers?

6. In the meantime the gospel is spreading to Gentiles at a tremendous rate in Antioch as a result of the believers who were scattered because of persecution. What kind of care is provided for new believers (vv. 22-30)?

7. What was Barnabas like, according to this passage?

8. How does our care for new believers compare and contrast to the care given here?

9. In this passage, how do you see the true meaning of *Christian* being more fully discovered and lived out in a multicultural church?

10. In what ways do you see your church resisting being a multicultural church?

embracing it?

11. What steps will you take to develop a relationship with a believer of another culture or ethnicity?

to help your church become more multicultural?

 Ask the Lord to help you be more open and flexible to the changes that he desires to bring about in your life. Ask him for patience and compassion with others with whom you sense change needs to take place.

NOW OR LATER

In the face of change, how do you handle the need for a new perspective? resistance? excitement? uncertainty? fear?

In what areas of your life and Christian community do you face change now? How are you responding to this change?

TWELVE

MIRACULOUS ESCAPE

Acts 12

Hudson Taylor, famous missionary to China, said, "Man is moved by God through prayer alone." The power of God is demonstrated in response to the prayers of his people.

Group Discussion. How have you seen God respond to a group of people who were earnestly praying?

Personal Reflection. Recall a time when God answered one of your prayers. Describe the joy of receiving his gracious blessing upon you.

Read Acts 12.

1. Describe how each character responds to what is happening.

2. What seems to motivate Herod's actions (vv. 1-5)?

3. Consider a time when you have acted wrongly for the sake of pleasing someone. What were the consequences of your actions?

4. What does the church's response to James's death and Peter's being in prison (vv. 5 and 12) demonstrate about prayer?

5. How quickly and persistently do you and your Christian community resort to prayer?

6. Put yourself in Peter's sandals. What would have gone on in your heart and mind during your rescue from prison?

7. Why do you think the praying Christians reacted as they did to Peter's return?

8. When have you been like those who told Rhoda, "You're out of your mind" (v. 15)?

9. Why was Herod struck down (vv. 21-23)?

10. Contrast Herod's end with what happened with the Word of God (vv. 19-24).

11. The earnest prayer of the church significantly affected the outcome of events in this chapter. How is your motivation to pray influenced by this truth?

 Ask the Holy Spirit to create in you a heart for prayer.

NOW OR LATER

Summarize Acts 1–12. Make three columns on a sheet of paper. In the first column list the themes of the chapters. In the second column list what you have learned about these themes. In the third, list how you have been influenced to become more committed as a follower of Jesus.

LEADER'S NOTES

My grace is sufficient for you.

2 CORINTHIANS 12:9

L eading a Bible discussion can be an enjoyable and rewarding experience. But it can also be *scary*—especially if you've never done it before. If this is your feeling, you're in good company. When God asked Moses to lead the Israelites out of Egypt, he replied, "O Lord, please send someone else to do it"! (Ex 4:13). It was the same with Solomon, Jeremiah and Timothy, but God helped these people in spite of their weaknesses, and he will help you as well.

You don't need to be an expert on the Bible or a trained teacher to lead a Bible discussion. The idea behind these inductive studies is that the leader guides group members to discover for themselves what the Bible has to say. This method of learning will allow group members to remember much more of what is said than a lecture would.

These studies are designed to be led easily. As a matter of fact, the flow of questions through the passage from observation to interpretation to application is so natural that you may feel that the studies lead themselves. This study guide is also flexible. You can use it with a variety of groups—student, professional, neighborhood or church groups. Each study takes forty-five to sixty minutes in a group setting.

There are some important facts to know about group dynamics and encouraging discussion. The suggestions listed below should enable you to effectively and enjoyably fulfill your role as a leader.

PREPARING FOR THE STUDY

1. Ask God to help you understand and apply the passage in your own life. Unless this happens, you will not be prepared to lead others. Pray too for the various members of the group. Ask God to open your hearts to the message of his Word and motivate you to action.

2. Read the introduction to the entire guide to get an overview of the entire book and the issues which will be explored.

3. As you begin each study, read and reread the assigned Bible passage to familiarize yourself with it.

4. This study guide is based on the New International Version of the Bible. It will help you and the group if you use this translation as the basis for your study and discussion.

5. Carefully work through each question in the study. Spend time in meditation and reflection as you consider how to respond.

6. Write your thoughts and responses in the space provided in the study guide. This will help you to express your understanding of the passage clearly.

7. It might help to have a Bible dictionary handy. Use it to look up any unfamiliar words, names or places. (For additional help on how to study a passage, see chapter five of *How to Lead a LifeGuide Bible Study*, Inter-Varsity Press.)

8. Consider how you can apply the Scripture to your life. Remember that the group will follow your lead in responding to the studies. They will not go any deeper than you do.

9. Once you have finished your own study of the passage, familiarize yourself with the leader's notes for the study you are leading. These are designed to help you in several ways. First, they tell you the purpose the study guide author had in mind when writing the study. Take time to think through how the study questions work together to accomplish that purpose. Second, the notes provide you with additional background information or suggestions on group dynamics for various questions. This information can be useful when people have difficulty understanding or answering a question. Third, the leader's notes can alert you to potential problems you may encounter during the study.

10. If you wish to remind yourself of anything mentioned in the leader's notes, make a note to yourself below that question in the study.

LEADING THE STUDY

1. Begin the study on time. Open with prayer, asking God to help the group to understand and apply the passage.

2. Be sure that everyone in your group has a study guide. Encourage the group to prepare beforehand for each discussion by reading the introduction to the guide and by working through the questions in the study.

3. At the beginning of your first time together, explain that these studies are meant to be discussions, not lectures. Encourage the members of the group to participate. However, do not put pressure on those who may be hesitant to speak during the first few sessions. You may want to suggest the following guidelines to your group.

- Stick to the topic being discussed.
- Your responses should be based on the verses which are the focus of the discussion and not on outside authorities such as commentaries or speakers.
- These studies focus on a particular passage of Scripture. Only rarely should you refer to other portions of the Bible. This allows for everyone to participate in in-depth study on equal ground.
- Anything said in the group is considered confidential and will not be discussed outside the group unless specific permission is given to do so.
- We will listen attentively to each other and provide time for each person present to talk.
- We will pray for each other.

4. Have a group member read the introduction at the beginning of the discussion.

5. Every session begins with a group discussion question. The question or activity is meant to be used before the passage is read. The question introduces the theme of the study and encourages group members to begin to open up. Encourage as many members as possible to participate, and be ready to get the discussion going with your own response.

This section is designed to reveal where our thoughts or feelings need to be transformed by Scripture. That is why it is especially important not to read the passage before the discussion question is asked. The passage will tend to color the honest reactions people would otherwise give because they are, of course, supposed to think the way the Bible does.

You may want to supplement the group discussion question with an icebreaker to help people to get comfortable. See the community section of *Small Group Idea Book* for more ideas.

You also might want to use the personal reflection question with your group. Either allow a time of silence for people to respond individually or discuss it together.

6. Have a group member (or members if the passage is long) read aloud the passage to be studied. Then give people several minutes to read the passage again silently so that they can take it all in.

7. Question 1 will generally be an overview question designed to briefly survey the passage. Encourage the group to look at the whole passage, but try to avoid getting sidetracked by questions or issues that will be addressed later in the study.

8. As you ask the questions, keep in mind that they are designed to be used just as they are written. You may simply read them aloud. Or you may prefer to express them in your own words.

There may be times when it is appropriate to deviate from the study guide. For example, a question may have already been answered. If so, move on to the next question. Or someone may raise an important question not covered in the guide. Take time to discuss it, but try to keep the group from going off on tangents.

9. Avoid answering your own questions. If necessary, repeat or rephrase them until they are clearly understood. Or point out something you read in the leader's notes to clarify the context or meaning. An eager group quickly becomes passive and silent if they think the leader will do most of the talking.

10. Don't be afraid of silence. People may need time to think about the question before formulating their answers.

11. Don't be content with just one answer. Ask, "What do the rest of you think?" or "Anything else?" until several people have given answers to the question.

12. Acknowledge all contributions. Try to be affirming whenever possible. Never reject an answer. If it is clearly off-base, ask, "Which verse led you to that conclusion?" or again, "What do the rest of you think?"

13. Don't expect every answer to be addressed to you, even though this will probably happen at first. As group members become more at ease, they will begin to truly interact with each other. This is one sign of healthy discussion.

14. Don't be afraid of controversy. It can be very stimulating. If you don't resolve an issue completely, don't be frustrated. Move on and keep it in mind for later. A subsequent study may solve the problem.

15. Periodically summarize what the group has said about the passage. This helps to draw together the various ideas mentioned and gives continuity to the study. But don't preach.

16. At the end of the Bible discussion you may want to allow group members a time of quiet to work on an idea under "Now or Later." Then discuss what you experienced. Or you may want to encourage group members to work on these ideas between meetings. Give an opportunity during the session for people to talk about what they are learning.

17. Conclude your time together with conversational prayer, adapting the prayer suggestion at the end of the study to your group. Ask for God's help in following through on the commitments you've made.

18. End on time.

Many more suggestions and helps are found in *How to Lead a Life-Guide Bible Study*, which is part of the LifeGuide Bible Study series.

COMPONENTS OF SMALL GROUPS

A healthy small group should do more than study the Bible. There are four components to consider as you structure your time together.

Nurture. Small groups help us to grow in our knowledge and love of God. Bible study is the key to making this happen and is the foundation of your small group.

Community. Small groups are a great place to develop deep friendships with other Christians. Allow time for informal interaction before and after each study. Plan activities and games that will help you get to know each other. Spend time having fun together—going on a picnic or cooking dinner together.

Worship and prayer. Your study will be enhanced by spending time praising God together in prayer or song. Pray for each other's needs— and keep track of how God is answering prayer in your group. Ask God to help you to apply what you are learning in your study.

Outreach. Reaching out to others can be a practical way of applying what you are learning, and it will keep your group from becoming self-focused. Host a series of evangelistic discussions for your friends or neighbors. Clean up the yard of an elderly friend. Serve at a soup kitchen together, or spend a day working on a Habitat house.

Many more suggestions and helps in each of these areas are found in *Small Group Idea Book.* Information on building a small group can be found in *Small Group Leaders' Handbook* and *The Big Book on Small Groups* (both from InterVarsity Press). Reading through one of these books would be worth your time.

STUDY 1. ACTS 1. YOU WILL BE MY WITNESSES.

PURPOSE: To understand the task of the church of Jesus Christ and his promise to equip us for that task.

Group Discussion. Every study begins with a group discussion question, which is meant to be asked before the passage is read. These questions are important for several reasons. First, they help the group to warm up to each other. Second, these questions get people thinking along the lines of the topic of the study. Most people will have lots of different things going on in their minds (dinner, an important meeting coming up, how to get the car fixed) that will have nothing to do with the study. Third, they can reveal where our thoughts or feelings need to be transformed by Scripture.

Question 1. As you lead the group in discussion about what Luke reported about Jesus' last days on earth, do not overlook the topics that Jesus discussed with his disciples—the kingdom of God and the Holy Spirit (vv. 3-5). It can be concluded that Jesus would talk about that which was of greatest importance to him as he spends his last days and hours with them.

Question 2. The book of Acts is a sequel to the Gospel of Luke. The Gospel of Luke is also addressed to Theophilus, whose name means "dear friend who loves God." As it says in verse 1, the book of Acts continues from where Luke left off in his Gospel. There is a lot of content covered in these eleven verses. This question is meant to give the group an understanding and overview of that material, as well as a grasp of the magnitude of all that has taken place.

It is important to look closely at all the evidence that there is in this orderly account. It is written by a professional, a physician, a person who is used to a scientific approach to data. Jesus had shown himself frequently and given many convincing proofs that he was alive. Luke is also strong on retelling powerful personal stories, which gives his account flavor and appeal.

Question 4. We are indeed given the task of being Jesus' witnesses throughout the world. The purpose of this question is to "feel" the awesomeness of the task as first presented to the apostles . . . and for that awesomeness to penetrate us as we continue in the task.

Question 5. There is the obvious equipping by the Holy Spirit being given to them. This should not be passed over lightly in discussion. What does it mean to have the Holy Spirit present and active in our lives and witnesses? How much do we recognize and depend on him?

Question 7. The promise that Jesus will return gives hope and purpose, which also equips us for the task of being effective witnesses.

Question 8. First, as is very understandable, they are described as "looking intently up into the sky as he was going" or "gazing up into Heaven," as the King James Version puts it (v. 10). Then, they somehow move toward a state of normalcy by going back home to Jerusalem, a three-quarter-mile walk. The walk probably helped in giving them time to talk and allow all that had just taken place to settle in. Ultimately their response was to gather together and pray.

Question 9. The most important aspect of being together was obedience. In verses 4-5 the report was that Jesus told them not to leave Jerusalem but to wait for the gift his Father promised them, the Holy Spirit. Being together also provided the opportunity for fellowship, encouragement and unity. We need one another.

Question 11. It would build their confidence greatly to see again that some of these remarkable things that were happening to them were written down many years before they had happened. David was an important patriarch. The direction came from the instructions that were in the quoted passage (Ps 69:25; 109:8).

STUDY 2. ACTS 2. RECEIVING THE POWER.

PURPOSE: To begin to understand the power of the Holy Spirit and the way he equips us for the task of being witnesses throughout the world.

General note. In chapter one the promise of the Holy Spirit is made by the risen Lord. The mission for his church is clearly defined. In chapter two this promise is fulfilled. It is the power of the Holy Spirit that enables the apostles to be "witnesses first in Jerusalem."

Questions 1-2. Help the group to use their imaginations and place themselves in the circumstances as much as possible. They need to remember all that had gone on over the past couple of months, from the crucifixion to the ascension, and the emotional as well as spiritual impact of it all for the disciples. Those in the crowd undoubtedly had been aware of much of what was going on, are confused and now face more.

Question 4. Educated Jews would know the Old Testament. Hearing Peter preach from the book of Joel and the Psalms would be important to them. The fact that what was happening before their eyes was written about years and years ago in the Scriptures they recognized as the Word of God was vital.

"Having established the Scriptural basis for what was happening, Peter went on to utilize and exemplify the very gift that was being given" (Lloyd J. Ogilvie, *The Communicator's Commentary: Acts* [Waco, Tex.: Word, 1983], p. 70).

Question 5. In the two cited verses Peter addresses "Fellow Jews" and "Men of Israel," in spite of the fact that there are people from many places in the crowd, as is stated in verses 9-11. Peter apparently had not yet caught the vision of worldwide evangelization that was presented in 1:8. We will see in later chapters of Acts how Peter's awareness and perspective change.

Question 6. Theophilus, by hearing about Peter's sermon through the author Luke, was exposed to Scripture being fulfilled (vv. 17-21, 25-28). When we directly see God doing what he says he will do, we are reassured that the object of our faith is true.

Question 7. Allow time for reflection and honesty. Do not be afraid of silence as people consider this important question. Be prepared to tell the group your response to this question.

Question 9. Many of us wonder how present and active the Holy Spirit is in our lives and ministries. So this is an important question worth spending time on. It also is important to know that the work of the Spirit is not just the dramatic demonstrations.

Question 12. This question is meant to touch at one of the longings of many believers today. It is a concept worth discussing. You might use such follow-up questions as "When have you experienced true fellowship?" or "How accessible is true fellowship to you?" or "Why is it lacking so today?" during this question or question 13.

STUDY 3. ACTS 3. HEALING POWER.

PURPOSE: To deepen our understanding of the power of God by seeing it demonstrated in the healing of the crippled beggar.

Group discussion. Sometimes "religious" non-Christians are the least open to hearing about Jesus. At other times the fact that they are religious is a sign of their hunger for and openness to the truth. One of my most exciting experiences of introducing people to Jesus through Bible study was in an adult Sunday school class. In the class were people who came to church because of a genuine hunger and openness, though many of them were not Christians.

Question 2. The beggar immediately began praising God. The crowd, on the other hand, suspected that Peter and John might have been directly responsible for this miracle. Peter was on guard and quickly addressed this matter and drew their attention to Jesus.

Question 3. Try to keep this question from "should respond" to how they do respond. Part of the discussion would consist of asking, what are amazing works of God? Some things that we take for granted are truly amazing. Part of the discussion might be how much do I expect to see God do amazing things? How open are my eyes to his amazing works? Do I want to experience the amazing works of God?

Question 4. The Jews observed three times of prayer: nine o'clock in the morning, three o'clock in the afternoon and sunset. At these times God-fearing Jews and devout Gentiles went to the temple to pray. It would be an ideal place to find those who were open to the truth about Jesus.

"The continued loyalty of the converted Jews to the temple services was mentioned in 2.46; here, then, are Peter and John proceeding thither and finding occasion for action and word in the name of Jesus (6)" (R. V. G. Tasker, *The Acts of the Apostles,* Tyndale New Testament Commentaries [Grand Rapids, Mich.: Eerdmans, 1980], p. 62).

Question 5. "In charging them Peter echoes the contrasts woven into the Isaiah prophecies. God glorified His Servant; the Jews betrayed Him (13). Pilate acquitted Him; the Jews denied Him (13). He was the Holy One and the Just; the Jews chose a murderer (14). The Jews killed Him; God raised Him from the dead (15)" (Tasker, *Acts of the Apostles,* pp. 63-64).

Question 7. "Complete healing" suggests spiritual and emotional healing as well as physical healing. Give time and encouragement so that people can share where they need God's healing. This could be a source of great pain.

Question 8. "After the manner of his first sermon, Peter turns, at verse 17, from stern denunciation to appeal. Let them repent, for their vast evil has not frustrated God. Christ's passion was in God's purpose. Verse 18 should be translated 'His Christ' and that is 'His anointed'. It is a quotation from Ps. 11:2, which Peter uses again in fuller form in iv. 26. Christ is still the living and the coming Savior, as the resurrection shows (19-21). Peter's main concern is to remove the Jews' stumbling block. The first and most necessary step in this Jewish evangel was to prove from the testimony of the prophets that the sufferings of the Messiah were part of God's plan. The argument from verses 19-25 may sound to western ears a trifle remote, but it would be illuminating and cogent to minds trained in the thought-forms and language of the Old Testament" (Tasker, *Acts of the Apostles,* pp. 63-64).

Questions 10-11, 13. Help the group to personalize this passage by sharing from their own experiences times of people being open to the truth about Jesus and how the power of God is demonstrated in their lives. It would be very helpful if you begin by sharing from your own experience as a leader.

Question 12. The power of the Holy Spirit is demonstrated as the truth about Jesus is proclaimed by the apostles. In verses 1-10, before the man is healed (through the power of the Holy Spirit), the truth about the source of the gift—and that it was a gift better than money—is proclaimed. In verses 11-13, again, the source of the power is identified. If the apostles had lied and taken credit for it, the power would not have been demonstrated.

Throughout the rest of the chapter, the truth about Jesus is proclaimed, and the power of the Holy Spirit is demonstrated throughout the book of Acts.

STUDY 4. ACTS 4:1-31. CALLED INTO QUESTION.

PURPOSE: To understand how the power of God equips us to be his witnesses throughout the world.

Question 2. "The apostles are technically on their defence, but actually they have gone over to the attack; Peter proceeds to preach the gospel to his judges, and he does so by citing a well known OT scripture. 'The stone which the builders rejected has become the head of the corner' (Psalm 118:22) is one of the earliest messianic testimonies. It was so used (by implication) by Jesus Himself, as the conclusion of the Parable of the Vineyard (Mark 12:10). In the original OT context the rejected stone is perhaps Israel, despised by the nations but chosen by God for the accomplishment of His purpose. But, as in so many other instances, the purpose of God for Israel finds its fulfillment in the single-handed work of Christ" (F. F. Bruce, *The Book of Acts,* The New International Commentary on the New Testament [Grand Rapids, Mich.: Eerdmans, 1974], pp. 99-100).

"Peter, bold as ever, pressed home his accusation where it most properly belonged, warning the supreme court that the same name by which the cripple had received bodily health was the *only* name through which they could receive from God spiritual health. This boldness was the more surprising on the part of 'laymen,' untrained in the rabbinical schools; but these men had been disciples of no ordinary teacher, who had Himself excited the surprised comment: 'How is it that this man has learning, when he has never studied?' (Jn. 7:15)" (G. J. Wenham, J. A. Motyer, D. A. Carson and R. T. France, eds., *New Bible Commentary,* 3rd ed. [Downers Grove, Ill.: InterVarsity Press, 1970], p. 977).

Question 3. You might need to help the group members think through even subtle criticisms as well as the cultural intolerance to anything or anyone who speaks of absolute truth.

Question 5. They saw the courage and boldness of Peter and John in proclaiming the gospel. The fact that they were "unlearned men" added to the potency of their stand. They probably remembered the same quality of Jesus' teaching just weeks prior, and they noticed the influence of Jesus on them—"they took note that these men had been with Jesus." It was also hard to stop them because they refused to obey people instead of God.

The evidence of what they claimed stood in their midst in the form of the healed man. Everyone in Jerusalem knew they had done an outstanding miracle that the religious leaders could not deny. The man who was miraculously healed was over forty years old, an age at which such cures just simply did not occur. All the people were praising God, and the religious leaders were afraid of them.

"This was the first mistake which the Jewish leaders made with regard to the new sect. And this mistake was fatal. There was probably no need to arrest the Nazarenes, thus calling attention to them and making them 'martyrs.' But once arrested, they should not have been freed so quickly. The arrest and release increased the number of believers; for these events showed on the one hand that the new sect was a power which the authorities feared enough to persecute, and on the other hand they proved that there was no danger in being a disciple of Jesus (he, of course, being the one who had saved them from the hand of their persecutors!)" (J. Klausner, *From Jesus to Paul*, trans. William F. Stinespring [New York: Macmillan, 1943], pp. 282ff.).

In summary, there was boldness in proclamation of the truth, even by unlearned men. There was the fact that the disciples "had been with Jesus." There was the undeniable evidence of the truth of their message, a healed man, a life that was changed. There was the commitment of obedience to God rather than people, and the fact that what they did and taught was in the name of Jesus.

Question 6. Help the group to look carefully at the responses to question 5 and then to discuss this question thoroughly.

Question 9. Graciously, God has given us the body of believers as a resource to witness to the world and a place to demonstrate the power of the Holy Spirit. His desire for his body is that they would be one. That oneness, that unity, allows for his power to flow freely.

Question 10. You may want to encourage the group to explore the definition of *sovereign*: "Above or superior to all others; chief, greatest, supreme. Supreme in power, rank or authority. Holding the position of reigning. A person who possesses supreme authority" (*Webster's New World Dictionary*).

"The two apostles, on their release, returned to the place where the other apostles were, and when they reported their experience before the Sanhedrin, the whole company resorted to prayer. They addressed God as Sovereign Lord, the Creator of all, in time-honoured language derived from Hebrew scripture" (Bruce, *Book of Acts,* pp. 105-6).

Question 12. "The Sanhedrin might threaten, but their threats called not for fear and silence but for increased boldness of speech. The apostles therefore prayed that they themselves might have courage to proclaim their message without fear or favour, and that God would place the seal of His public approval on their witness by granting further mighty works of healing and similar signs and wonders through the same name which had cured the lame man—the name of His 'holy Servant Jesus'" (Bruce, *Book of Acts,* pp. 106-7).

STUDY 5. ACTS 4:32–5:16. ONENESS OF HEART.

PURPOSE: To observe the unity of the church as an expression of the power of the Holy Spirit.

Question 2. "The spirit-filled community exhibited a remarkable unanimity, which expressed itself even in the attitude to private property. Each member regarded his private estate as being at the community's disposal: those who possessed houses and lands sold them in order that they might be more conveniently available to the community in the form of money. The richer members thus made provision for the poorer, and for a time no one had any room to complain of hunger and want. The apostles, as the community leaders, received the free-will offerings that were brought, but they apparently delegated the details of distribution to others, for they themselves had to devote their time and energy to their public testimony to the risen Christ. As they did so, the power of God shown in mighty works, attended their preaching the very thing for which they had prayed (vs. 30). And they continued to enjoy the grace of God and the Jerusalem populace" (Bruce, *Book of Acts,* pp. 108-9).

Question 5. This is a speculative question. Allow the group to brainstorm and investigate how they might feel if they observed such an incident.

Question 6. "The sovereign presence of the Holy Spirit is so real that any action done to the church is regarded as done to the Spirit, just as any action taken by the church is predicated of the Spirit" (*New Bible Commentary,* 3rd ed., p. 978). This narrative emphasizes the Spirit's indwelling presence in the church and the practical and solemn implications of that.

Question 7. Be sure to give this question the time it needs to help the group evaluate how "lying" takes place. It is an important issue and can be subtle. We can lie by speaking half-truths, by sharing information about others that we do not know is truth (not that knowing it is true automatically makes it all right to share), pretending that we are something that we are not, refusing to admit failure or confess sin, and so on.

Question 8. Truth and integrity are basic to trust, and without trust a community withers and dies.

Question 10. They probably feared a fate like that of Ananias and Sapphira. They may also have feared the kind of persecution the apostles were facing. Notice that verse 13 says no one "dared join them," but verse 14 says that more believers were added. This probably means they lost observers or fringe folk and added only committed believers.

Question 11. The Christian church is often not held in high regard in the unbelieving world. Much of that is our fault. Some problems include the way we treat each other, the way we treat sinners in the world, the unloving way in which we often communicate truth about Jesus and the way we live as a people full of pride instead of full of humility. Jesus said, "By this will all people know that you are my disciples by the way you love each other."

Question 12. It is important not to slide by this question because of similar questions in past studies. Christian community is important, and you need to help the group look at the unique and specific characteristics of the church or Christian community in this particular passage in order to understand them and then to evaluate their own community based on this passage.

STUDY 6. ACTS 5:17–6:7. PERSECUTION & EXPANSION.

PURPOSE: To consider the total inadequacy of those who attempted to thwart the growth of the church of Jesus Christ through opposition and persecution, and to observe how the church continued to expand.

Question 1. This is an overview question. It is to help your group get a grasp of the events of this passage. Move the group through the passage without getting bogged down with details. Do, however, consider the more covert episodes of emotion as well as the more obvious. For example, after discussing the more obvious, ask such follow-up questions as: "How do you think the apostles felt as the angel 'opened the doors of the jail and brought them out' (5:19)?" What might the officers have felt when they arrived at the jail and found the apostles gone (5:22)? Often what is demonstrated emotionally is not the full story of what is going on in hearts and minds.

"The apostolic healing mission provoked the second attack by the authorities, much as the healing of the congenital cripple had provoked the first. Angered by the failure of their first assault on the apostles, dismayed to see that they had ignored the court's prohibition and threats, and *filled with jealousy* (17) of their power and popularity, *the high priest and all his associates, who were members of the party of the Sadducees* resolved to take further action.

"This time they arrested not only Peter and John but *the apostles,* most if not all of them (see 29), and *put them in the public jail (18)*" (John R. W. Stott, *The Message of Acts,* The Bible Speaks Today [Downers Grove, Ill.: InterVarsity Press, 1990], pp. 113-14).

"It was the popularity of the Christians that filled the Jewish leaders with *jealousy* and prompted them to action, rather than the mere fact of the connection with Jesus. They were not, at this stage, persecuted because they were Christians but because they were successful. . . .

"Most of the Sanhedrin could see only the implication that they were being accused by unlearned people claiming to have divine authority, and thus they were *furious and wanted to put them to death*" (*New Bible Commentary*, 4th ed., pp. 1075-76).

Question 2. What happened to the apostles is dramatic. This kind of dramatic situation is not necessary for members of your group to respond to this question and to apply what we are learning to their lives and churches. Some questions that might help are: What situations in your life are calling for difficult, consistent obedience? In what situations of proclaiming the gospel do you need the peace of the Holy Spirit? perseverance? Are there relationships in your life in which clear proclamation of the good news of Jesus is needed, even if it is rejected? What decisions do you need to make to obey God rather than follow a cultural norm?

Question 3. "Gamaliel is a name known to us from Jewish as well as Christian sources as a teacher of the law, who was honoured by all the people. It is perhaps significant that he was a Pharisee, whereas at this stage in the church's history it seems it was the Sadducees who were the more determined opponents (5:17; see also 4:1). Gamaliel was a student of one of the greatest rabbis of all times, Hillel, and he was Paul's tutor (22:3). This great man seems to have taken the point of the apostles' 'reversal' statements, and he advocated taking the apostles at their word and allowing similar principles to settle the current dispute: these Christians have argued that God's ruling in the case of Jesus overturned the human judgment. Then let God decide in this case as well. Gamaliel was of course, confident that God was not on the side of the Christians and that, therefore, nothing would come of their movement, just as nothing had come of the two rebellions that he mentioned" (*New Bible Commentary*, 4th ed., p. 1076).

Question 4. His message was "God is over all. Let these men go, and we will see if they are of God." It strikes me that the fact that Gamaliel's words—the words of an unbeliever—were used to persuade them to spare the apostles lives is an example of "God's being over all."

Question 8. They listened to the needs of the people, and they acted. They delegated the work. They gave criteria for choosing the men. They recognized the spiritual nature of the work of the seven and laid their hands on them. The Twelve did not try to do it all themselves. They knew their call was to give attention to the ministry of the Word and prayer.

Question 9. Help the group to not slide over this application question, but look carefully at what the apostles modeled and how that can be applied to their churches and to themselves.

Question 11. Look at both the positive and negative responses.

STUDY 7. ACTS 6:8–7:60. SPIRIT & WISDOM.

PURPOSE: To consider God's Spirit and wisdom in Stephen and to seek to make them more a part of our lives.

General note. As you prepare to lead your group through this passage, ask God to work in the group for them to desire to be filled with the Holy Spirit and his wisdom.

Question 1. Allow a few minutes for the group to scan the passage and get to know Stephen. You might ask such follow-up questions as: What does it mean to be "full of grace and power"(v. 8)? What do you think was significant about "his face being like the face of an angel"? What impact would this have on the crowd? Describe the way that he proclaimed truth (vv. 51-53). What were his character and spirit like (vv. 59-60)?

You certainly do not want to use all these questions. You may not need any of them. It depends how well your group gets into knowing and experiencing Stephen on their own and how much help they need.

Question 2. Encourage the members of your group to get into this passage experientially through this question.

Question 3. Stephen reminds us of Jesus. Throughout the Gospels, people are amazed at the wisdom and authority Jesus spoke with. "Stephen expounded the implications of this messiahship more radically than his fellow-believers. . . . They accepted his premises (for like him they acknowledged the authority of Old Testament scripture), but they could not accept his conclusions, so scandalous and revolutionary did they appear" (Bruce, *Book of Acts,* pp. 133-34).

Question 4. Stephen's understanding of spiritual worship does not depend on the ceremonial law or the temple. This is why the charges were brought against him. He was more farsighted than the other leaders in Christianity in his comprehension of the break with Judaic worship that Christianity brought with it. In this he blazed the trail for Paul and the writer of Hebrews.

> The Twelve had kept the respect and goodwill of the Jerusalem populace; they attended the Temple services regularly, and appeared outwardly to be observant Jews whose only distinction from others was that they believed and proclaimed Jesus to be the Messiah. . . .
>
> His speech is a reasoned exposition of his teaching about the transitory nature of the Jewish worship. An attack on the temple, as Stephen's teaching was construed to be, ranked as blasphemy of the worst kind; there was also the subordinate consideration that the economy of Jerusalem was based on the temple. The rulers at once saw their opportunity, and arraigned Stephen on a popular charge. (*New Bible Commentary,* 3rd ed., p. 979)

Question 5. Stephen's defense is a review of the history of Israel. It takes the form of a historical retrospect—a form well established in Jewish tradition. He introduces the content of his response to the accusations: the building of Solomon's temple and the giving of the law on Mt. Sinai. The refusal of their forefathers to obey Moses, the fact that their forefathers had the tabernacle in the desert and were able to worship there, and the fact that God cannot be maintained in a particular place are other important points.

Question 8. "The third part of the speech concerns the temple proper. If he was charged with speaking against the temple and the customs of Moses, as if those were two permanent features of Judaism, Stephen reminded his audience that precisely those two features were at variance with each other. The temple itself was a change to the customs handed down by Moses (6:14), which concerned a tabernacle built at God's direction. This was a change tolerated, but not initiated, by God. Stephen was no more against Judaism than the Jewish Scripture itself, as expressed through the prophet *Isaiah, who he quoted (Is. 66)"* (*New Bible Commentary,* 4th ed., p. 1077).

Question 9. "It was rather Stephen's audience who were against the prophets, the Holy Spirit who spoke through them and the Messiah whose coming they predicted. Stephen closed with this fierce attack: it was his audience who should be on trial for violating the spirit of Judaism, not him" (*New Bible Commentary,* 4th ed., pp. 1077-78).

Questions 11-12. Make sure there is time to discuss these questions and that they are not just tacked on. Also, allow time to pray about what is learned.

STUDY 8. ACTS 8. THE POWER OF SUFFERING.

PURPOSE: To observe the expansion of the church in the midst of persecution and suffering, and to integrate into our lives the principles of evangelism that are observed in this process.

Question 1. "The persecution and dispersion, however, brought about a beginning of the fulfillment of our Lord's commission to His disciples in Ch. 1:8, 'ye shall be my witnesses both in Jerusalem, and in all Judaea and Samaria.' 'The churches of God which are in Judaea in Christ Jesus' (to borrow Paul's language in 1 Thes. 2:14) were born in this time of persecution" (Bruce, *Book of Acts,* p. 175).

Because of the disdain of the Jews for the Samaritans, it was a bold act on Philip's part to proclaim the good news to the Samaritans. The Samaritans did however share with many of the Jews the hope of the coming Messiah.

"Peter and John were sent to Samaria to find out whether or not the Samaritans were truly becoming believers. The Jewish Christians, even the apostles, were still unsure whether Gentiles (non-Jews) and half Jews could receive the Holy Spirit. It wasn't until Peter's experience with Cornelius (chapter 10) the apostles became fully convinced that the Holy Spirit was for all people" (*The Life Application Bible* [Wheaton, Ill.: Tyndale House, 1962], p. 1636).

Question 2. Give the group time to think if they do not respond to this question immediately. Try to lead an honest discussion of this question. For those who have been Christians for a while, this question might seem old and not be taken seriously. For new believers it might be one of the first times they have considered this command, at least as an important part of their lives.

Be prepared to share honestly from your own experience, positive as well as negative. Often a question like this brings out where we have failed. To talk about where God is working and where members of the group are experiencing being witnesses is vital and motivating.

Question 3. Do not overlook the work that the Spirit did in Philip in a more quiet way as well as the more dramatic acts of the Spirit of God.

Question 4. "Concerning Simon the following should be noted: His faith was concerned with miracles (13, 19, 20), and ended in amazement, not holiness; his view of God was materialistic. 'Simony' became a term for traffic in sacred things. Gehazi is the Old Testament parallel and perhaps Balaam (2 Peter 2:15); his aim was self-aggrandizement; he was afraid (24), but not visibly repentant. Simon disappears at this point from the story, but in legend he has a lurid career of magic and wizardry. Peter's words (23) are the key to Luke's emphasis on the story, and a 'root of bitterness' (Dt. xxix.18) Simon's tribe have indeed been in the Church" (Tasker, *Acts of the Apostles,* p. 80).

Question 5. The way to receive God's power is to ask God's forgiveness, turn from sin and receive the Holy Spirit. God's power comes from repentance and belief in Christ as Savior. This is quite opposite to the world's view of receiving power.

Question 7. There is some debate as to the authenticity of Simon's conversion. Help the group to not spend too much time in this type of debate, but rather move more deeply through the principles discussed here.

Philip appears to have accepted this man's discipleship, and indeed his professed adherence to the Church may have been set down as a remarkable conversion. This is where he began. Whether his conversion was real or not, the principles of discipleship and confrontation are important. Redemption is a process, and Simon had much to be redeemed from in his old life, assuming the conversion was real.

Question 9. "Ethiopia was located in Africa south of Egypt. The eunuch was obviously very dedicated to God because he came such a long distance to worship in Jerusalem. The Jews had contact with Ethiopia in ancient days (Psalms 63:31; Jeremiah 38:7), so this man may have been a Gentile convert to Judaism. Because he was the treasurer of Ethiopia, his conversion brought Christianity into the power structures of another government. This is the beginning of the witness 'to the ends of the earth' (1:8). Isaiah had prophesied that Gentiles and eunuchs would be blessed (Isaiah 56:3-5)" (*Life Application Bible,* p. 1636).

Question 11. Have the group scan back through the passage to look for the kinds of evangelism. This question is not as important as the next. The purpose of the question is to observe the fact that God certainly works in all kinds of ways and all types of situations. It also is to encourage your group members to think through how they most effectively can communicate the gospel.

Question 12. Cover this question thoroughly. Remember such things as the vital, indispensable role of the Holy Spirit in conversion and in leading you to opportunities where people are ready to hear and respond to the gospel. Obedience to his voice is vital. Also, the place of the Word is important in communicating the faith. And there is much more.

STUDY 9. ACTS 9:1-31. SAUL'S CONVERSION.

PURPOSE: To consider God's miraculous work in Saul's conversion and the effect of this on the whole church.

Question 1. "The narrative now returns to Saul of Tarsus and his campaign of repression against the Christians, which received brief mention in 8:3. He was not content with driving them from Jerusalem; they must be pursued and rooted out wherever they fled, not only within the frontiers of the land of Israel but beyond them as well. 'In raging fury against them'—to quote his own words at a later time—'I persecuted them even to foreign cities' (Ch. 26:11, RSV)'" (Bruce, *Book of Acts,* p. 193).

The high priest was in charge of the internal affairs of the Jewish state. His authority was upheld by the Roman power. His decrees were binding to a great degree in Jewish communities outside Palestine.

Someone in the group may have a question about the use of the phrase "the Way." "The name by which Christianity here is described, 'The Way' (v 2) recurs in Chs. 19:9, 23; 22:4; 24:14, 22. That was evidently a term used by the early Christians to denote their own movement, considered as the way of life or the way of salvation" (Bruce, *Book of Acts,* p. 194).

Question 2. Paul himself gave one consistent account of this encounter with Christ. In that one illuminating flash he saw the glorified Christ, and in the voice that followed he heard Christ speak.

"The more one studies the event, the more one agrees with the eighteenth century English statesman, George Lyttelton, that 'the conversion and apostleship of St. Paul alone, duly considered, was of itself a demonstration sufficient to prove Christianity to be a divine revelation'" (Bruce, *Book of Acts*, p. 196).

Question 3. This may seem like a strange question. Few conversions happen like Saul's. However, to look at his to compare and contrast it with ours is a way to closely examine our own conversion and the miracle of God's grace on our lives.

You may have some in your group who have not been converted. This question will give them an opportunity to hear the stories of others and to ask any questions they wish.

Question 4. Help the group to look carefully at these two encounters with the Lord. Comparison and contrast are effective ways of doing this.

Examples of the contrasts include Saul asking, "Who are you, Lord?" while Ananias knew immediately who was calling him. The Lord asks Saul a question about Saul's response to him. But with Ananias the relationship is established, and he begins with instructions.

Examples of how the two encounters compare are that both respond with obedience. And questions were allowed and responded to by the Lord. Look carefully for others.

Question 5. It is especially hard to show love to those we fear or whose motives we doubt. Ananias was both afraid of and doubted Saul. Out of obedience to the Lord, he greeted Saul lovingly, even as a brother. He was accepted as one of the family of God.

Question 10. You might want to help your group think through what might have happened if Barnabas had not defended Saul to the believers who were afraid of him.

Question 11. Barnabas was one of the Jewish converts mentioned in 4:36. He became the bridge between Saul and the other Christians and apostles.

New Christians need help and support. They need people more experienced in the faith who will walk with them, teach, encourage and introduce them to other believers. Help the group to think through how this has happened to them and specifically how they can become this to young believers that they know or lead to the Lord. They should discuss how they would like to grow in this area and even set some goals.

STUDY 10. ACTS 9:32–10:48. SALVATION FOR EVERY NATION.

PURPOSE: To increase our understanding of the potential of the gospel to reach every person in all the corners of the world.

Question 2. Having been used of God to raise someone from the dead might make the impossibility of taking the gospel to the Gentiles more "possible."

Question 3. It is good to remember God's faithfulness in our lives. As we see him work, our faith and obedience grows. His work may be dramatic or quiet. The responses to this question should be encouraging to each of the group members.

Question 4. Here are thoughts from the *New Bible Commentary* (4th ed.):

Although it is likely that the Ethiopian eunuch was the first non-Jewish convert to Christianity (8:25-40), it was the conversion of Cornelius that sparked the controversy about Gentile converts among the Jewish Christians who probably had not heard about Philip and the eunuch. The account here suggests that the Christian community in general, and Peter in particular, were not prepared for the direct acceptance of Gentile converts and had to be convinced. Luke means us to see the acceptance of the situation by the church in ch 11 as forming the background for the later decision in ch 15.

The first scene in this complex story begins with an introduction of *Cornelius, and centurion*. This was a position of some limited authority. He served in the *Italian Regiment* of which we know little. A regiment or 'cohort' of 600 soldiers was divided into six 'centuries', with a centurion as the head of each.

Although he was a Roman soldier, *he and all his family were devout and Godfearing*. The term 'God-fearers' appears to have been frequently used for a class of people who believed, and to some extent followed, the Jewish religion without being fully converts to Judaism (see 13:16, 26; 17:4, 17 for this sense; the phrase 'worshipper of God' is probably referring to the same phenomenon; 16:14, 18:7). 'Fearing God' could also be used to describe someone as merely religious (so 2:5), but would seem redundant in this sentence if that was all it meant here. In short, this man and his family were not Jews nor Jewish converts, but were also no longer pagans worshipping other gods. (pp. 1081-82)

Question 7. In verse 14 Peter questions God. This happens three times. Peter wonders about the vision. In spite of uncertainty Peter invited the Gentiles into his home and went with them the next day. In verse 28 Peter reminds Cornelius that it is against Jewish law for him to associate with a Gentile. He shares what God has shown him from the vision. (He still seems skeptical.) Cornelius's explanation seems to increase Peter's understanding and he says, "I now realize *how true* it is that God does not show favoritism but accepts men from every nation who fear him and do what is right." Peter was then willing to share the message with the Gentiles, observe and acknowledge the outpouring of the Spirit on them and even initiate their being baptized (baptism constitutes their entry into the Christian church).

Question 8. Cornelius was expecting them; he invited friends and relatives in and received Peter with great respect.

Question 9. From the story of Cornelius, we can learn that God reaches those who want to know him. The gospel is for all people. There are people who are eager to believe everywhere. Help the group to dig and answer thoroughly.

Question 10. See 10:9-48. Trace carefully all that God does for Peter in this process of taking the gospel to the Gentiles.

Question 12. The gospel was spread to Gentiles, and the first Gentile church was established. Also Cornelius was responsible for one hundred soldiers and would probably be returning to Rome soon; his conversion was a major steppingstone for spreading the gospel to the capital city.

STUDY 11. ACTS 11. THE FIRST JEWISH-GENTILE CHURCH.

PURPOSE: To observe how the church is progressing from a Jewish church separate from the Gentiles to a Jewish-Gentile fellowship.

Question 1. Encourage discussion by such follow-up questions as, What do you think Peter felt? What would it have been like for you to walk into this situation?

Question 2. The group discussion question has prepared the group for this question by asking them to think about situations where they have been criticized. Now they have the opportunity to share what they are like when they experience this. Note this question is not what should you be like, but what *are* you like.

Question 3. Peter is matter-of-fact and not defensive. He shared all the details and told them precisely how it happened. He was honest and vulnerable about his own questions and doubts. And he shared his deep conviction about what God had done—"So if God gave them the same gift as he gave us, who believed in the Lord Jesus Christ, who was I to think that I could oppose God?" (v. 17).

Question 6. The early church was very conscientious about nurturing their new believers. In this passage Barnabas is sent up to Antioch when news reached the church in Jerusalem that people were turning to the Lord. As he saw what needed to be done, he got more help. He went after Saul in Tarsus. They met with the church at Antioch for a whole year.

Question 7. In verses 22-26 Barnabas is described as sensitive to, and glad for, God's grace and work. He was encouraging and full of the Holy Spirit and faith. He was persistent and thorough.

> The leaders of the Jerusalem church recognized the novelty of the situation at Antioch when news of it reached them, and just as Peter and John had earlier gone to Samaria to investigate Philip's missionary service there, so now Jerusalem sent a delegate to Antioch to look into the strange events that were being enacted in that great city. It was a critical moment; much—far more than they could have realized—depended on the delegate whom they chose to send. In the providence of God, they chose the best man for this delicate and important work—Barnabas, the "son of

encouragement." Barnabas himself was a Cypriote Jew by birth, like some of those who had begun to preach the gospel to the Antiochene Gentiles, and his sympathies would in any case be wider than those of Jewish Christians who had never set foot outside Judaea. (Bruce, *Book of Acts*, p. 240)

Question 8. Too often today conversions, rather than disciples, is the emphasis. When a person is newly born into the kingdom of God our work has just begun. Just as a physical infant needs care, nurture, feeding—all their needs provided for in order for them to grow and be healthy—so it is with baby Christians. The leaders in the early church took this responsibility seriously.

Question 10. Change within a local congregation can be fearful for some. Keeping it the way it has always been is an important goal. Changing for the sake of change is not necessary. But change for the gospel's sake is important. Sensitive evaluation of this, along with loving and compassionate encouragement for needed change, is important.

Question 11. To be sure, we have the same biases as the early Jewish church had. We just have different starting points. Help your group discuss these in light of what our Christian response should be.

STUDY 12. ACTS 12. MIRACULOUS ESCAPE.

PURPOSE: To deepen our understanding of the power of God as we see it demonstrated in the escape of Peter from prison, by Herod's death and in the increase and spread of the Word of God even in the midst of great opposition.

Question 1. Help the group to look carefully at the people and to notice little details like Peter sleeping soundly in prison while Herod had four men at a time guard him. (Notice Peter's peace in comparison to Herod's fear and apprehension.)

Question 2. "During his brief reign over Judea (41-44), Herod, despite his faults, proved a studious patron of the Jewish faith, and maintained friendly relations with the religious leaders of the people. It is said that on one occasion, when reading the law at the Feast of Tabernacles, he burst into tears as he read Dt. 17:15 ('one from among your brethren you shall set as king over you; you may not put a foreigner over you, who is not your brother'), for he remembered the Edomite origin of the Herod family; but the populace cried out: 'Be not distressed; you are our brother!'

"His execution of James the Zebedean, and his arrest of Peter, are related here. The words, 'he saw that it pleased the Jews,' are significant, for reasons already suggested" (*New Bible Commentary*, 3rd ed., p. 987).

> Herod's attack on the church was no doubt a policy move to gratify and conciliate the old Pharisaic and Sadducean enemies of the church. The persecution, therefore, and the imprisonment of Peter recorded in this chapter, follow in direct sequence the events narrated in X. I-XI 18. The zealous observance, which had heretofore marked the Jerusalem church, had gone far to allay the fears of the religious leaders.
>
> Provided Christianity remained within the strict Jewish fold, and confined its activities to the framework of the old faith, the Sadducees had no fault to find with it, and the Pharisees found no cause for complaint. But Peter's report caused alarm which spread beyond the confines of the Church. Vested interests took fright, and, either directly persuaded, or sensing an opportunity, the king started this petty persecution. (Tasker, *Acts of the Apostles,* p. 99)

Question 4. Prayer was important to the early Christians. They believed God heard them in their need and that they were dependent on God. It demonstrates trust and dependence.

Question 6. "Peter was in the custody of four soldiers at a time, of whom two were probably on guard at either side of him and two at the door" (*New Bible Commentary*, 3rd ed., p. 987).

Question 8. There are times that God does unusual things or answers prayers in dramatic ways and allows us to see them. The response of others to this could be, in so many words, "You are out of your mind," that is, "That can't be." When has this happened to you?

Question 10. "The persecutor dies; the cause he persecuted survives in increasing vigor" (*New Bible Commentary*, 3rd ed., p. 988).

Phyllis J. Le Peau worked with InterVarsity Christian Fellowship for over two decades in St. Louis and the Chicago metro area. She is also the author of the several Bible study guides published by Zondervan and InterVarsity Press, including the LifeGuide Bible Studies Grandparenting, Love, *and* Women of the New Testament. *She and her husband, Andy, have four married children and thirteen grandchildren.*

WHAT SHOULD
WE STUDY NEXT?

Since 1985 LifeGuide® Bible Studies have provided solid inductive Bible study content with field-tested questions that get groups talking— making for a one-of-a-kind Bible study experience. This series has more than 120 titles on Old and New Testament books, character studies, and topical studies. IVP's LifeGuide Finder is a great tool for searching for your next study topic: https://ivpress.com/lifeguidefinder.

Here are some ideas to get you started.

BIBLE BOOKS

An in-depth study of a Bible book is one of the richest experiences you could have in opening up the riches of Scripture. Many groups begin with a Gospel such as Mark or John. These guides are divided into two parts so that if twenty or twenty-six weeks feels like too much to do as once, the group can feel free to do half of the studies and take a break with another topic.

A shorter letter such as Philippians or Ephesians is also a great way to start. Shorter Old Testament studies include Ruth, Esther, and Job.

TOPICAL SERIES

Here are a few ideas of short series you might put together to cover a year of curriculum on a theme.

Christian Formation: *Christian Beliefs* (12 studies by Stephen D. Eyre), *Christian Character* (12 studies by Andrea Sterk & Peter Scazzero), *Christian Disciplines* (12 studies by Andrea Sterk & Peter Scazzero), *Evangelism* (12 studies by Rebecca Pippert & Ruth Siemens).

Building Community: *Christian Community* (10 studies by Rob Suggs), *Friendship* (10 studies by Carolyn Nystrom), *Spiritual Gifts* (12 studies by Charles & Anne Hummel), *Loving Justice* (12 studies by Bob and Carol Hunter).

GUIDES FOR SPECIFIC TYPES OF GROUPS

If you have a group that is serving a particular demographic, here are some specific ideas. Also note the list of studies for seekers on the back cover.

Women's Groups: *Women of the New Testament, Women of the Old Testament, Woman of God, Women & Identity, Motherhood*

Marriage and Parenting: *Marriage, Parenting, Grandparenting*